MW00823656

Conversation Planner for Kids with Autism & Asperger's

Six-Minute Conversation Skills

Happy Frog Press

Copyright 2019 by Janine Toole PhD

All rights reserved. This book or any portion thereof

may not be reproduced or used in any manner whatsoever

without the express written permission of the publisher

except for the use of brief quotations in a book review.

First Printing, 2019

ISBN 978-1-989505-10-6

Happy Frog Press

www.HappyFrogPress.com

Table of Contents

Introduction

Welcome to the **Conversation Planner** workbook! Inside you'll find easy-to-use worksheets that teach a step-by-step method to prepare for any conversation or social situation.

Your student will learn to think about who they are talking to, what that person will expect, when to know the person is ready for the conversation, etc. Conversation Planner gives your child the tools to complete successful conversations.

Students begin with multiple choice answers, but progress to independent thinking. By the end of the workbook, your students will be able to think, discuss and be prepared for any conversation. A great achievement!

How to Coach a Six-Minute Session

No student wants to spend extra time learning. Follow the guidelines in this section to promote efficient and motivating progress for your student.

1. Have a consistent and regular schedule

Consistency and regularity are vital if you want to reach a goal. So, choose a regular schedule for your six-minute sessions, get your learner's agreement and stick to it!

In a school setting, make this task a regular part of your students' day. In a home setting, aim for 3-4 times per week.

2. Devise a reward system

Working on skill deficits is hard work for any learner. Appreciate your student's effort by building in a reward system.

This may include a reward when a specific number of exercises are finished, when tasks are completed correctly on the first try, or whatever specific goal will encourage your learner at this point in their journey.

Remember to reward based on effort as well as correctness.

3. Most importantly....

Most importantly, make this a FUN experience with your learner!

Learning happens best when our brains are relaxed - not stressed. It is your job to make sure your student's brain stays ready to learn while doing this workbook. Build success upon success and celebrate every small achievement.

Key Idea 1:

Who is Your Talking Partner?

TALKING PARTNER

Every conversation includes you and someone you are talking to.

This person is your **talking partner**.

Talking Partner

You are at a park and you see your friend Kian, who you haven't seen in two years.

Who is your talking partner?

Kian

My mom

You want to check the weather on your dad's phone, but he is in a hurry.

Who is your talking partner?

My mom

My dad

Talking Partner

You and your cousin Marie have 2 hours to wait to catch a plane.

Who is your talking partner?

Marie

The pilot

You are at the animal shelter and you want to know if there are any dogs for adoption.

Who is your talking partner?

The dogs

The shelter worker

Talking Partner

You are at the gift-wrapping station at the mall to get a gift wrapped.

Who is your talking partner?

You are at the school library and you want to return an overdue book and pay the fine.

Who is your talking partner?

Talking Partner

You are late for school and you need to explain why you are late to the school secretary.

Who is your talking partner?

Your brother is playing on the iPad, but you want a turn.

Who is your talking partner?

Key Idea 2:

What is Your Conversation Goal?

CONVERSATION GOAL

Your conversation goal is the reason why
you are having a conversation.

Conversation Goal

You and your friend Jake have just finished karate class and now you are walking home together.

What is your conversation goal?

To argue

To talk with Jake about things we are interested in

While you are walking to school, your friend Tim rides by on a bike. You call out and say, "Hi!"

What is your conversation goal?

To have a long talk with Tim

To be friendly to Tim

Conversation Goal

You are very early for art class, so you are talking to your instructor.

What is your conversation goal?

To talk about things my instructor is interested in

To learn something about science.

You are at a restaurant and the waiter gave you the wrong meal. You call him back.

What is your conversation goal?

To learn about what the waiter is interested in

To get the meal I ordered

Conversation Goal

It is the first day of summer camp and you have 10 minutes to get to know the boy sitting next to you.

What is your conversation goal?

You notice your friend Lily in the checkout line at the supermarket. You are in a hurry to get milk.

What is your conversation goal?

Conversation Goal

You and your family attend a big family reunion.

What is your conversation goal?

You are on the bus to the city center and you need to ask the driver which stop to get off at.

What is your conversation goal?

Key Idea 3:

What is Your Partner's Conversation Goal?

YOUR PARTNER'S CONVERSATION GOAL

Your talking partner might have a different conversation goal than you.

Partner's Conversation Goal

You and your friends are on your way to a concert and you see your uncle who is working at the concert.

What is your uncle's goal?

To say 'Hi' but to keep working.

To spend an hour chatting with you.

While you are waiting at the vet, the lady next to you asks about your cat.

What is the lady's goal?

To pass time while she is waiting

To learn about your cat for a test

Partner's Conversation Goal

You and your friend Keshia are playing basketball and talking in the back yard

What is Keshia's conversation goal?

To talk about things that interest us both

To talk only about her interests

You need to ask a sales assistant the price of a pen you want to buy.

What is the sales assistant's goal?

To help me make a purchase.

To learn things about me.

Partner's Conversation Goal

You come into the library and an old lady asks you if it is raining outside.

What is the old lady's goal?

You are in the electronic shop to return some headphones you bought a few days ago.

What is the sales assistant's goal?

Partner's Conversation Goal

At the Pancake House you ask the waiter to refill your bottomless iced tea.

What is the waiter's goal?

Your teacher Ms Jackson is getting on the bus just as you are getting off. She says, "Hi."

What is Ms Jackson's goal?

Conversation Planner Review 1

> You and your friend are at a Korean restaurant. You have just finished ordering.

Who is your talking partner?

_____

What is your conversation goal?

_____

What is your talking partner's goal?

_____

Conversation Planner Review 1

> You are in line at the coffee shop and it is your turn to order.

Who is your talking partner?

_____

What is your conversation goal?

_____

What is your talking partner's goal?

_____

Conversation Planner Review 1

You are visiting your Aunt Steffy and her new baby in hospital.

Who is your talking partner?

_____

What is your conversation goal?

_____

What is your talking partner's goal?

_____

Key Idea 4:

Who Else Is Nearby?

OTHER PEOPLE NEARBY

Sometimes there are other people nearby who can be affected by your conversation. In this section you think about who else might be affected by your conversation.

Other People Nearby

You want to buy some aspirin at a drugstore.

Who else is nearby?

Other shoppers at the drugstore

Your aunt

You are waiting in line outside your classroom.

Who else is nearby?

Other classmates

A bus driver

Other People Nearby

You are in a cafeteria and you want to ask the server about today's lunch menu.

Who else is nearby?

Other people in line at the cafeteria

The janitor

You are talking with your friend at the mall.

Who else is nearby?

Other shoppers at the mall

Builders

Other People Nearby

You see your favorite football player and you want to take a selfie with him.

Who else is nearby?

You need to ask the shop assistant if you can return the phone you are thinking of buying.

Who else is nearby?

Other People Nearby

You are walking to school and you see your neighbour Mr Peterson on the other side of the street.

Who else is nearby?

You are at the cinema and you see your sister's friend.

Who else is nearby?

Key Idea 5:

What Are Other People's Goals?

OTHER PEOPLE's GOALS

Other people have expectations about your conversation, too. Let's find out what they might be.

Other People's Goals

You are on the bus and you ask the person next to you what the time is.

What expectations do other people have?

That they won't be disturbed by your conversation

To join in your conversation

You are at the pharmacy and you need to ask what cough medicine would be best for your mom. There are other people waiting.

What expectations do other people have?

That you will finish your conversation quickly

That you will ask their question for them

Other People's Goals

Your mom's plane is late, and you go ask at the landing gate what the cause of the delay is.

What expectations do other people have?

To get the answers they need from the airline staff.

To get a free ticket

You are at the museum and you see your favorite movie star. You want to say, "Hi."

What expectations do other people have?

To get a turn to talk to the movie star.

To interrupt you

Other People's Goal

You are at a music store and you want to buy your favorite band's latest album.

What expectations do other people have?

You are at the beach and you ask your friends to mind your things while you go swimming.

What expectations do other people have?

Other People's Goals

You are at the coffee shop and you plan to order hot chocolate.

What expectations do other people have?

Your friend introduces you to his cousin when you bump into her at the mall.

What expectations do other people have?

Conversation Planner Review 2

You need to ask your teacher, Mr Wong, for permission to go to the bathroom.

Who is your talking partner?

_____

What is your conversation goal?

_____

What is your talking partner's goal?

_____

Who else is nearby?

_____

What expectations do other people have?

_____

Conversation Planner Review 2

You are at the bowling alley and you want to ask if there are lanes free.

Who is your talking partner?

_____

What is your conversation goal?

_____

What is your talking partner's goal?

_____

Who else is nearby?

_____

What expectations do other people have?

_____

Conversation Planner Review 2

> You have a message to give to the school secretary.

Who is your talking partner?

_____

What is your conversation goal?

_____

What is your talking partner's goal?

_____

Who else is nearby?

_____

What expectations do other people have?

_____

Key Idea 6:

Should This Be A Short Conversation?

SHORT CONVERSATIONS

Some situations need a short conversation that stays focused on one topic.

Ordering a drink at a coffee shop is an example of a situation that needs a short conversation.

Short Conversations

You are fishing at the lake with your dad.

Does this need a short conversation?

Yes

No

You have a question for the museum tour guide.

Does this need a short conversation?

Yes

No

Short Conversation

You and your mom are waiting for your sister to try on a few dresses.

Does this need a short conversation?

| Yes | No |

You need to call the vet to make an appointment.

Does this need a short conversation?

| Yes | No |

Key Idea 7:

Should This Be A Long Conversation?

LONG CONVERSATIONS

Some situations are more relaxed and have time for a longer conversation with several topics.

Spending time with your friend is an example of a good situation for a longer conversation.

Long Conversations

You and your grandparents are playing a board game in the living room.

Do you have time for a longer conversation?

Yes	No

You are at the cinema and you want to buy two tickets to a movie.

Do you have time for a longer conversation?

Yes	No

Long Conversations

You are at the school library and you want to return an overdue book.

Is this the time for a longer conversation?

Yes	No

You are sitting around a campfire with other members of your Scout group.

Do you have time for a longer conversation?

Yes	No

Conversation Planner Review 3

> You and your friend Keyla are looking at fancy dresses at the mall.

Who is your talking partner?

_____

What is your conversation goal?

_____

What is your talking partner's goal?

_____

Who else is nearby?

_____

What expectations do other people have?

_____

What type of conversation is best: long or short?

_____

Conversation Planner Review 3

The bell rings just as you see that your friend Max has a new haircut.

Who is your talking partner?

_____

What is your conversation goal?

_____

What is your talking partner's goal?

_____

Who else is nearby?

_____

What expectations do other people have?

_____

What type of conversation is best: long or short?

_____

Conversation Planner Review 3

Your mom introduces you to her friend's daughter who is your age. She is interested in Pokémon like you.

Who is your talking partner?

_____

What is your conversation goal?

_____

What is your talking partner's goal?

_____

Who else is nearby?

_____

What expectations do other people have?

_____

What type of conversation is best: long or short?

_____

Key Idea 8:

Is Your Talking Partner Ready For The Conversation?

STARTING CONVERSATIONS

Before you can start a conversation, you need to know the other person is ready. You use your eyes and your ears to see if your talking partner is ready.

Ready to Start

You want to buy some candy at the corner store.

How will you know the cashier is ready to talk to you?

She is looking at me.

She is talking to another customer.

You are at the mall with your best friend looking at video games.

How will you know your friend is ready to talk to you?

She is talking to someone else.

Her body is facing towards me.

Ready to Start

You are at the pet store and you have a question about dog food.

How will you know the sales assistant is ready to talk to you?

The assistant is talking to another customer

The assistant looks at me and smiles.

You will have a Skype chat with your grandfather.

How will you know your grandfather is ready to talk to you?

My granddad is on camera and looking at me.

The connection is not ready.

Ready to Start

At the playground, you see the friendly dog sitter who took care of your dog last summer.

How will you know the dog sitter is ready to talk to you?

You are at a restaurant with your parents.

How will you know your parents are ready to talk to you?

Ready to Start

You are at a park and you see your friend Kian, who you haven't seen in two years.

How will you know Kian is ready to talk to you?

At the bus stop you want to ask the man next to you what the time is.

How will you know the man is ready to talk to you?

Key Idea 9:

How to Start A Conversation

STARTING CONVERSATIONS

Let's practice how to start conversations. It will be different each time depending on who you are talking to and what your goal is.

Starting the Conversation

You are waiting in line with your friend Linden outside your classroom. Linden likes basketball.

What is a good conversation starter?

Are you playing basketball tonight?

I need to get my hair cut.

You are riding your bike to the corner store and you see your gym teacher, Ms Clarke.

What is a good conversation starter?

Hi, Ms Clarke!

Bye!

Starting the Conversation

You just saw a very funny movie with your sister and now you are walking home together.

What is a good conversation starter?

Which bus are you catching?

That movie was hilarious!

You are at the school library and you want to return an overdue book.

What is a good conversation starter?

I hate reading.

I need to return an overdue book.

Starting the Conversation

You are waiting with a classmate at the bus stop.

What is a good conversation starter?

You are at the pet store and you want to know which type of dog food to buy.

What is a good conversation starter?

Starting the Conversation

You are at the museum with your family and you see your school principal.

What is a good conversation starter?

You are on your way to school and you see your elderly neighbour Mrs Kim.

What is a good conversation starter?

Key Idea 10:

How To Finish A Conversation

FINISHING CONVERSATIONS

It is important to know how to finish a conversation. Let's practice.

Finishing a Conversation

On the way to music class, you want to wish your friend Sofia a happy birthday.

How can you finish the conversation?

I hope you have a fun day!	Did you get a lot of presents?

The librarian just helped you find a book.

How can you finish the conversation?

Walk away without saying anything.	Say, "Thanks," and move away.

Finishing a Conversation

You need to ask your math teacher for permission to hand in your math assignment late.

How can you finish the conversation?

I hate math.

Thanks for the extra time.

You chat with your neighbor Bryan at the dog park, but now you need to go.

How can you finish the conversation?

Nice talking to you. See you later.

Walk away without saying goodbye.

Finishing a Conversation

> You are at your cousin's wedding and you have just congratulated them. Many people are waiting to do the same.
>
> How can you finish the conversation?

> You are studying at the library with your classmate, but now you need to go home.
>
> How can you finish the conversation?

Finishing a Conversation

You are at your friend's house and you just asked your friend's mom if you can use the phone. She said yes.

How can you finish the conversation?

You and your grandma are playing a board game, but now you have to go do some homework.

How can you finish the conversation?

Conversation Planner Review 4

> Your mom introduces you to her friend's daughter who is your age. She is interested in Pokémon like you.

Who is your talking partner?

_____

What is your conversation goal?

_____

What is your talking partner's goal?

_____

Who else is nearby?

_____

What expectations do other people have?

_____

Conversation Planner Review 4

What type of conversation is best: long or short?

_____

How will you know when your talking partner is ready?

_____

What is a good conversation starter?

_____

How can you finish the conversation?

_____

Conversation Planner Review 4

There is a new kid in your church group. You have been assigned to be her buddy.

Who is your talking partner?

_____

What is your conversation goal?

_____

What is your talking partner's goal?

_____

Who else is nearby?

_____

What expectations do other people have?

_____

Conversation Planner Review 4

What type of conversation is best: long or short?

_____

How will you know when your talking partner is ready?

_____

What is a good conversation starter?

_____

How can you finish the conversation?

_____

Key Idea 11:

How To Repair A Conversation

CONVERSATION REPAIR

Sometimes conversations can go wrong. Let's practice what to do when a conversation does not go smoothly.

Conversation Repair

You are at the animal shelter to adopt a dog. But the shelter worker thinks you want to adopt a cat.

How can you repair this conversation?

What are you talking about?

I want to adopt a dog, not a cat.

Your teacher wrote the wrong date on the board and you tell her. But your teacher thinks you want to know the date.

How can you repair this conversation?

You wrote the wrong date on the board.

Listen to me!

Conversation Repair

You and a grade 3 boy are talking while waiting for the bus after school. The boy thinks your name is 'Jim.'

How can you repair this conversation?

Are you stupid? I'm not Jim.

I'm Callam, not Jim.

You are at the library and you want to check out some books. But the librarian thinks you want to pay a fine.

How can you repair this conversation?

I just want to check out books today.

Fine? What fine?

Conversation Repair

You and your friend Caleb are watching YouTube videos. Caleb thinks you want to watch wrestling videos, but you don't.

How can you repair this conversation?

You want to buy some aspirin at the drug store. But your credit card doesn't work and you don't have any cash.

How can you repair this conversation?

Conversation Repair

You and your brother are waiting while your mom shops. Your brother thinks you said something rude to him. You didn't.

How can you repair this conversation?

While you are walking to school, your friend rides by on a bicycle. You call out, but he doesn't hear you.

How can you repair this conversation?

Key Idea 12:

What to Know/Bring

WHAT TO KNOW/BRING

Some conversations need you to decide things ahead of time or to bring something with you. Let's practice thinking about that!

What to Know/Bring

You plan to buy lunch at the cafeteria.

What should you bring or know before you start?

Your homework

Money to pay

You are at a restaurant and the waitress give you the wrong meal.

What should you bring or know before you start?

The meal you ordered

The cost of the meal

What to Know/Bring

You are in an electronics store to return a defective headset you bought a few days ago.

What should you bring or know before you start?

Your music player

The receipt

You are at the library to borrow a book.

What should you bring or know before you start?

Library card

Money to pay

What to Know/Bring

You are at the pet store and you don't know what sort of dog food to buy.

What should you bring or know before you start?

You are at the library and you want to put a book on hold.

What should you bring or know before you start?

What to Know/Bring

You are at a busy coffee shop and plan to order something.

What should you bring or know before you start?

You are at the cinema and you will buy some tickets.

What should you bring or know before you start?

Conversation Planner Review 5

> You are trying to convince your mom to come on a class field trip. She doesn't want to go.

Who is your talking partner?

_____

What is your conversation goal?

_____

What is your talking partner's goal?

_____

Who else is nearby?

_____

What expectations do other people have?

_____

Conversation Planner Review 5

What type of conversation is best: long or short?

_____

How will you know when your talking partner is ready?

_____

What is a good conversation starter?

_____

How can you finish the conversation?

_____

If needed, how can you repair the conversation?

_____

What should you know/bring ahead of time?

_____

Conversation Planner Review 5

You are at the gift-wrapping station at the mall. You want them to wrap a birthday present for your friend.

Who is your talking partner?

_____

What is your conversation goal?

_____

What is your talking partner's goal?

_____

Who else is nearby?

_____

What expectations do other people have?

_____

Conversation Planner Review 5

What type of conversation is best: long or short?

_____

How will you know when your talking partner is ready?

_____

What is a good conversation starter?

_____

How can you finish the conversation?

_____

If needed, how can you repair the conversation?

_____

What should you know/bring ahead of time?

_____

Conversation Planner Review 5

You are at the hair salon and you need to ask if you can get a haircut today.

Who is your talking partner?

_____

What is your conversation goal?

_____

What is your talking partner's goal?

_____

Who else is nearby?

_____

What expectations do other people have?

_____

Conversation Planner Review 5

What type of conversation is best: long or short?

_____

How will you know when your talking partner is ready?

_____

What is a good conversation starter?

_____

How can you finish the conversation?

_____

If needed, how can you repair the conversation?

_____

What should you know/bring ahead of time?

_____

Conversation Planner Review 5

At the mall, you can't find the shirt you want in your size. You need to ask the shop assistant for help.

Who is your talking partner?

_____

What is your conversation goal?

_____

What is your talking partner's goal?

_____

Who else is nearby?

_____

What expectations do other people have?

_____

Conversation Planner Review 5

What type of conversation is best: long or short?

_____

How will you know when your talking partner is ready?

_____

What is a good conversation starter?

_____

How can you finish the conversation?

_____

If needed, how can you repair the conversation?

_____

What should you know/bring ahead of time?

_____

Answer Key

Page 5	Kian	*My dad*
Page 6	Marie	*The shelter worker*
Page 7	Gift wrap employee	*Librarian*
Page 8	School secretary	*My brother*
Page 10	To talk with Jake about things we are interested in	*To be friendly to Tim*
Page 11	To talk about things my instructor is interested in.	*To get the meal I ordered.*
Page 12	To find out what the boy is interested in	*To say a quick hello to my friend.*
Page 13	To talk with different family members about what they have been doing.	*To find out where to get off.*
Page 15	To say 'Hi' but to keep working.	*To pass time while she is waiting.*
Page 16	To talk about things that interest us both.	*To help me make a purchase.*
Page 17	To find out if it is raining outside.	*To help you with your return.*
Page 18	To give you good service.	*To say hello without missing the bus*
Page 19	My friend,	*To talk with each other about things we are interested in.*
Page 20	Coffee shop worker	*To order my drink.* *To take my order and payment.*
Page 21	My aunt Steffy	*To congratulate her (or similar)*

88

		To introduce you to her new baby. (or similar)
Page 23	Other shoppers at the drug store	Other classmates
Page 24	Other people in the cafeteria line.	Other shoppers at the mall.
Page 25	Other people near the football player	Other people in the shop
Page 26	Other people on the street	Other people at the cinema
Page 28	That they won't be disturbed by your conversation.	That you will finish your conversation quickly.
Page 29	To get the answers they need from the airline staff	To get a turn to talk to the movie star.
Page 30	To not wait too long to get a turn.	To enjoy the beach without being disturbed.
Page 31	To get a turn to give their order without waiting too long.	To shop without being disturbed.
Page 32	Mr Wong.	Other students
	To get permission to go to the bathroom.	To not be disturbed by your request.
	To give permission without disturbing the rest of the class.	
Page 33	The worker at the bowling alley.	Other people who want to bowl.
	To find out if there are lanes free.	To get their turn quickly.
	To give you the information you need quickly.	
Page 34	The school secretary	Other students waiting.
	To give the information to the secretary.	To get their turn quickly.
	To get your information quickly.	
Page 36	No	Yes

Page 37	No	Yes
Page 39	Yes	No
Page 40	No	Yes
Page 41	Keyla To talk about things we are interested in.	Other people at the mall. To shop without being disturbed. Long
Page 42	Max To say something about Max's haircut. To get to class on time.	Other students To get to class on time. Short
Page 43	The friend's daughter. To be polite and get to know her. To be polite and get to know you.	Your mom and her friend. To have their own conversation. Long
Page 45	She is looking at me.	Her body is facing towards me.
Page 46	The assistant looks at me and smiles.	My granddad is on camera and looking at me.
Page 47	She is now talking to someone else. (or similar)	Your parents have decided what to order. (or similar)
Page 48	Kian is not talking to someone else. (or similar)	The man is not doing anything else. (or similar)
Page 50	Are you playing basketball tonight?	Hi, Ms Clarke!
Page 51	That movie was hilarious.	I need to return an overdue book.
Page 52	What book did you choose for your assignment? (or similar)	Hi, Can you help me choose the best food for my dog?
Page 53	Hi Mr P!	Hi, Mrs Kim!

Page 55	*I hope you have a fun day!*	*Say, "Thanks," and move away.*
Page 56	*Thanks for the extra time.*	*Nice talking to you. See you later.*
Page 57	*I hope you enjoy your day. I'll talk to you later.*	*I need to go. See you tomorrow.*
Page 58	*Thanks for letting me use the phone.*	*Thanks for the game. I have some homework, so I'd better get started on it.*
Page 59-60	*The daughter* *To talk to her about Pokémon and other things.* *To talk to me about Pokémon and other things.*	*My mom and her mom* *To have their own conversation* *Long* *When she looks at me.* *"Hi, What's your favorite Pokémon?"* *"Looks like Mom is going. Nice meeting you."*
Page 61-62	*The new kid* *To make him feel comfortable* *To meet new people* *Other kids* *To have a good time in church group*	*Long* *Hi. Did you just move to town?* *It's time for snack. Come on and I'll introduce you to other kids.*
Page 64	*I want to adopt a dog, not a cat.*	*You wrote the wrong date on the board.*
Page 65	*I'm Callam, not Jim.*	*I just want to check out books today.*
Page 66	*I don't like Wrestling. Can we watch some Minecraft videos?*	*Uh oh. My credit card isn't working. I'll have to go get some cash.*
Page 67	*You must have misheard me. I didn't say anything ride.*	*I can call out again.*

Page 69	Money to pay	The meal you ordered
Page 70	The receipt	Library card
Page 71	Information about your dog: age, bred, etc.	Library card and the name of the book.
Page72	What you want to drink. Money to pay.	The movie you want to see. Money to pay.
Page 73-74	My mom. To persuade her to go on the field trip. To no go on the field trip. Other members of the family. To not be disturbed. Short	She looks at me when I get her attention. Hi mom. I have a big favor to ask. Thanks, mom. You're the best. It's not this Tuesday. It's next Tuesday. Reasons why it is a good idea for my mom to go on the field trip.
Page 75-76	The gift wrap worker. To get my gift wrapped. To get my gift wrapped quickly. Other people in the gift wrap line To get a turn quickly. Short	She finished with the previous customer and looks at me. Could you wrap this in birthday paper please. It's for a ten year old girl. Thanks. It looks great. It's for a girl. Not a boy. Money to pay & the present.
Page 77-78	The salon receptionist. To get a haircut. To help you as a customer Other people in the salon To be helped and not disturbed. Short	She is not talking to anyone else and looks at me Hi, can you fit me in for a cut? Thanks. I'll come back at 3. I just need a cut. I don't need a blow dry. Ideas for how I want my hair cut. Money to pay.
Page 79-80	Shop assistant. To get the shirt in the right size.	She is not helping anyone else and looks at me.

To sell you a shirt.

Other shoppers.

To shop without being disturbed.

Short

Hi, do you have this in a size 10?

Thanks. Where do I pay?

I need a size 10, not a 12.

Money to pay. Know my own size.

Additional Resources

If you found this book useful, please leave a short review on Amazon. It makes an amazing difference for independent publishers like Happy Frog Press. Just two sentences will do!

And don't forget to check out the other book in our **Six-Minute Conversation Skills** series.

Your learners might also benefit from our **Six-Minute Social Skills series**.

The workbooks in this series build core social skills for kids who have social skills challenges, such as those with Autism, Asperger's and ADHD.

Although numbered, these books can be used in any order.

For extra support with comprehension and/or expressive language skills, take a look at the following books in the **Six-Minute Thinking Skills** series.

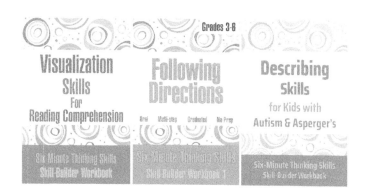

CERTIFICATE
OF
ACHIEVEMENT

THIS CERTIFICATE IS AWARDED TO

_____

IN RECOGNITION OF

_____

_____   _____

DATE   SIGNATURE

Made in the USA
Las Vegas, NV
12 January 2025

16255289R00057